# EMOJITELLS
## Digital Show & Tell

Children's Book
By Miss Mikka

Copyright © 2017 by Mekka Gay

All rights reserved. No part of this publication may be reproduced, distributed, or transmitted in any form or by any means, including photocopying, recording, or other electronic or mechanical methods, without the prior written permission of the publisher, except in the case of brief quotations embodied in critical reviews and certain other noncommercial uses permitted by copyright law.

ISBN: 978-0-692-94312-0

Illustrations by Dipali Dutta & Stefanysr
Book design by Stephanayr

First Printing:  2017
Club Millennial, LLC

Miss Mikka is a speaker, educator and journalist, who is passionate about social media education. She works as the Coordinator for the Bronx Community College Science and Technology Entry Program. One of her proudest moments was coaching her students to a first-place prize, in 2015, at the New York State STEP competition. The project, #HashtagsForJustice explored the role social media played in anti-violence police protests. In 2017, her students won again, taking second place for their project, Emojiverse. It explored whether emoji is a universal language. She is on a mission to continue educating the public about using social media responsibly, by providing training to schools and organizations through the consulting firm she started called, Club Millennial, LLC.

Explore her website: clubmillennial.com

Miss Mikka would like to dedicate this book to the students she has had the privilege of educating, along with her nephew and nieces, Liam, Makaia & Neysa.

There is a new form of show and tell. It gives you a chance to leave a trail. Cell phones and computers are used to post. You can share the things you like the most.

#CannotDelete

**IM...**
Explain what social media is used for and give examples. Show and Tell is a great analogy. Tell your child it's an opportunity to use technology to communicate ideas, opinions, and things with friends and family. Explain once you share, it cannot be erased.

**IM...**
Talk about sharing and having a good time,
but remember there are no secrets on social media.

**IM...**
Explain the importance of making wise choices.
Think about what you choose to share before you post it.

**IM...**
Explain the importance of adding friends and accepting requests.

**IM...**
Take advantage of sharing and staying connected with friends and family.
When you meet a new person you can stay in touch and continue to develop the friendship.

**IM...**
Social media may become part of your daily activities, but limit the time you spend online. Sometimes people get stressed by feeling the need to constantly respond to friends and comments. Do not feel bad or guilty if you decide to take time off.

**IM...**
When you use social media, be nice and positive to others.
You have a chance to make your friends feel good.

**IM...**
No one likes a bully. Do not tease or say mean things when using social media.
Everyone will know you are behaving badly.

**IM...**
You have a choice to make good or bad decisions on social media.
Be careful of the friends you accept and information you share.

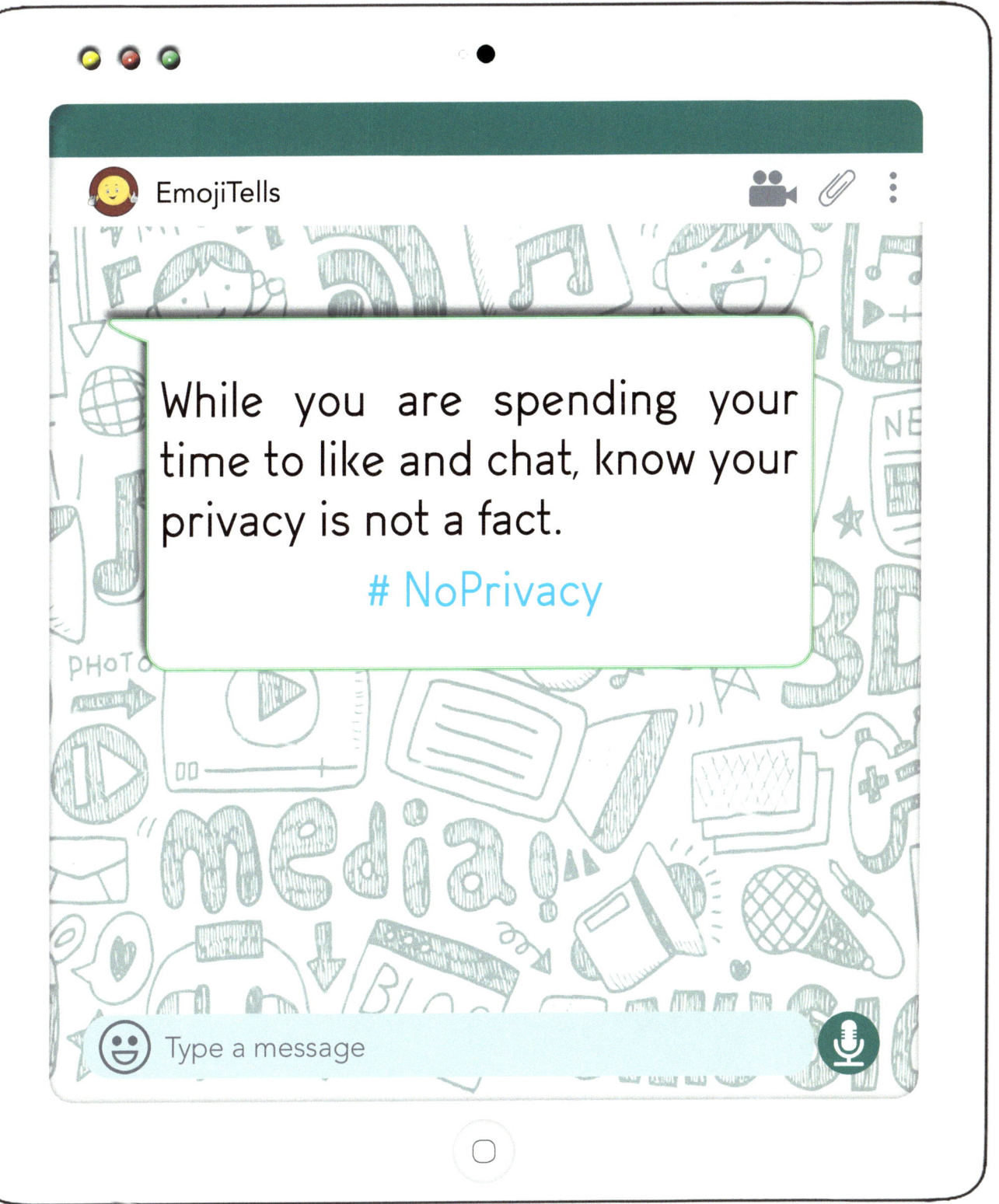

**IM...**
Social media is like a friend who cannot keep a secret.
Do not expect anything to be private.

**IM...**
Think before you post. Take at least 5 seconds and think about what good or bad things may happen if you decide to say something. Sometimes it is better to stay quiet.

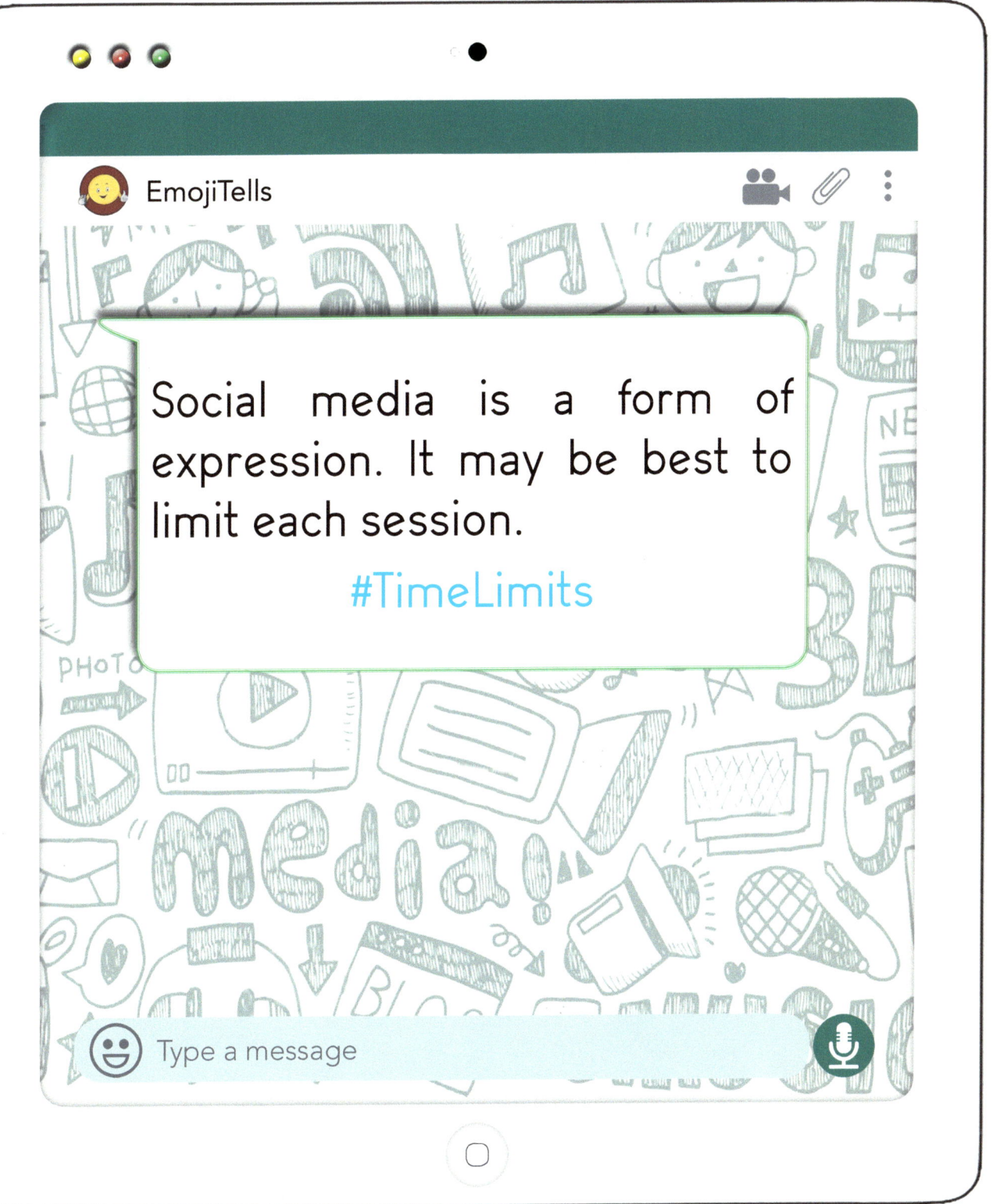

**IM...**
Don't spend all of your free time on social media.
Limit the time you spend online, instead take time to hang out with your friends.

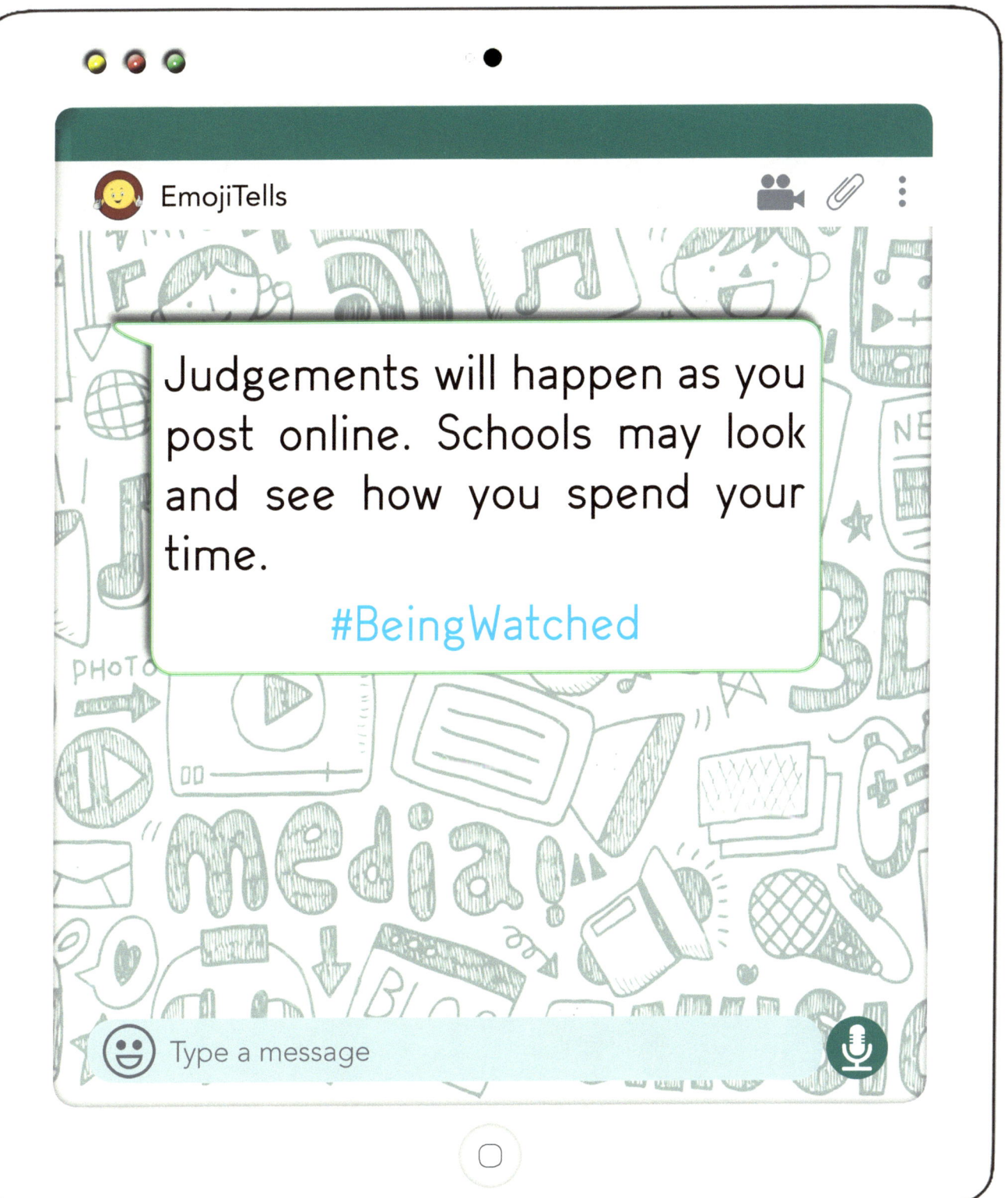

**IM...**
You are being watched when you use social media.
Parents, teachers, family members and the community will have opinions on the things you decide to post.

**IM...**
Keep in mind, you will make and lose friends on social media.
Some people may get mad about what you share or if you don't respond to them quickly.

**IM...**
Your real friends will be there and support you as you share.

www.ingramcontent.com/pod-product-compliance
Lightning Source LLC
LaVergne TN
LVHW071029070426
835507LV00002B/82